DOGS SET VI

SPRINGER SPANIELS

Nancy Furstinger
ABDO Publishing Company

visit us at
www.abdopub.com

Published by ABDO Publishing Company, 4940 Viking Drive, Edina, Minnesota 55435.
Copyright © 2006 by Abdo Consulting Group, Inc. International copyrights reserved in
all countries. No part of this book may be reproduced in any form without written
permission from the publisher. The Checkerboard Library™ is a trademark and logo of
ABDO Publishing Company.

Printed in the United States.

Cover Photo: Corbis
Interior Photos: Corbis pp. 7, 13, 15, 16, 19, 21; Getty Images pp. 8, 9; PhotoEdit p. 17;
    Ron Kimball pp. 5, 11

Series Coordinator: Megan M. Gunderson
Editors: Heidi M. Dahmes, Megan M. Gunderson
Art Direction: Neil Klinepier

Library of Congress Cataloging-in-Publication Data

Furstinger, Nancy.
    Springer spaniels / Nancy Furstinger.
        p. cm. -- (Dogs. Set VI)
    Includes bibliographical references.
    ISBN 1-59679-276-0
        1. English springer spaniels. 2. Welsh springer spaniels I. Title.

SF429.E7F87 2006
636.752'4--dc22
                                                    2005045735

CONTENTS

THE DOG FAMILY

More than 12,000 years ago, friendly wolf pups joined nearby humans. The pups soon began helping humans by hunting and guarding. And, they wiggled their way into hearts as the family pet. These early tamed animals developed into today's **domestic** dogs.

Now, almost 400 different **breeds** exist worldwide. Each dog has been bred for a special purpose, such as pulling sleds or hunting with their owners. And, dogs differ greatly in appearance. They come in many colors and sizes.

Despite their differences, all dogs belong to the **family** Canidae. This name comes from the Latin word *canis*, which means "dog."

Other members of the Canidae **family** are coyotes, foxes, jackals, and wolves. Dogs descended from wolves, and they still have similar qualities today. They both howl and growl to communicate. And, they share superior senses of smell and hearing.

Dogs may be bred to help with different tasks. But many dogs simply become well-loved companions for their owners!

SPRINGER SPANIELS

In the past, both springer spaniels and cocker spaniels appeared in the same **litters**. Littermates weighing more than 28 pounds (13 kg) were labeled springers.

These dogs spring at feathered game and flush them out of their hiding places. This is how they earned their name. There are English springer spaniels and Welsh springer spaniels. Today, they are recognized as two separate **breeds**.

Originally, the Welsh breed hunted along the coastlines of Wales, Ireland, and Scotland. They are superb retrievers, even in icy waters. So, Welsh springers became the favorite hunting dogs of nobles.

Springer spaniels became popular with American sports people during the late 1800s and early 1900s. In 1910, the English springer spaniel was recognized by the **American Kennel Club (AKC)**. The Welsh springer spaniel followed in 1914.

These spaniels are ready to hunt! They were probably trained to flush out game. This means they find the game and chase it from its hiding place.

What They're Like

Friendly and affectionate, springer spaniels make cheerful playmates. These dogs burst with curiosity and are always ready to go. They enjoy outdoor fun. They catch balls in city parks and swim in country lakes.

Many U.S. presidents have had their pets with them at the White House. Spot (left) and Barney (right) belong to President George W. Bush.

In the field, these gundogs flush out and retrieve game. They sniff out and trail pheasants and other land birds. And, they jump into ponds and marshes to fetch waterfowl.

Springer spaniels quickly learn commands. Positive obedience training can make lessons fun. And, these graceful dogs love to perform. They do well in dog shows because their smooth, strong stride makes them shine in the show ring.

This springer spaniel won a medal for helping save lives in Iraq.

COAT AND COLOR

The English springer spaniel's medium-length outer coat can be flat or wavy. The Welsh springer spaniel has a straight, soft, flat coat. Both spaniels have soft, short undercoats. The fur on the ears, legs, chest, belly, and tail is feathered.

The English coat comes in a variety of colors. It can be liver, or reddish brown, with white markings. It can also be black with white markings. Or, it can have black or liver markings on a white background. The coat can also be blue or liver roan.

Another possible color for an English springer is tricolor. This is black and white or liver and white, with tan markings.

The Welsh coat does not have as much variety. It is rich red and white only. White fur may be flecked

The springer spaniel's thick undercoat resists water and thorns. This is helpful for a hunting dog!

with red ticking, or markings. Any pattern that combines these two colors is accepted by the **AKC**.

The English springer spaniel's coat color determines if the nose is black or liver. The Welsh springer spaniel's nose can be black or a shade of brown. But, the nose may not be pink.

SIZE

Springer spaniels are medium-sized sporting dogs. The English male stands 20 inches (51 cm) high at the shoulders and weighs about 50 pounds (23 kg). The female is slightly smaller. She stands 19 inches (48 cm) high and weighs about 40 pounds (18 kg).

The Welsh **breed** is smaller and lighter. Males stand 18 to 19 inches (46 to 48 cm) high at the shoulders. Females stand 17 to 18 inches (43 to 46 cm) high. The average weight is 35 to 45 pounds (15 to 20 kg).

Springer spaniels have sporty, well-balanced bodies. They combine strength with endurance. Their hindquarters are muscular. And, their round feet have thick pads. The head ends in a square, straight **muzzle**.

Hundreds of years ago, this popular breed appeared in tapestries and paintings.

English ears are long, wide, and low set. They hang close to the cheeks. Welsh ears are smaller and don't quite reach the nose. English eyes are oval, and can be dark hazel, deep brown, or black. Welsh springers have dark to medium brown eyes.

CARE

A springer spaniel has a glossy coat that is groomed to look natural. Every day, use a brush to remove dead hair from your pet. It will also need regular baths, but not as often as its owner!

Unlike a pet dog, a show dog requires more specific grooming. Springers need to have the body and face hand-stripped. This is plucking the fur by hand. The coat should not be clipped.

A groomer can neaten your springer spaniel for the show ring. They can trim feathered areas with grooming scissors. They also remove excess hair from around the ears.

Besides a groomer, your springer spaniel also needs to visit a veterinarian. The veterinarian can **spay** or **neuter** your pet. And each year, your dog should receive a health checkup and **vaccines**.

A regular checkup with a veterinarian can help prevent a variety of health problems for any breed.

Owners should also keep an eye on their pet's teeth. Keep them clean using toothpaste and a toothbrush made specially for dogs.

FEEDING

Your new springer spaniel should arrive home with the same food it ate at the **breeder**'s. If you wish to change your dog's diet, slowly mix in the new food. This will prevent an upset stomach.

A dog bone can be a fun treat for your pet. But, make sure the bone is a safe size!

Your puppy will grow into a healthy dog by eating a good, balanced diet. Commercial dog food is available in dry, semimoist, and canned forms. The label should list a protein, such as chicken, as one of the first ingredients.

A feeding guide appears on the label of all dog foods. This guide matches the right amount of food to the age and weight of your dog. Many people prefer to feed their springer spaniels twice daily. And,

Just like their owners, dogs need to eat healthy food to help build strong bones and muscles.

most dogs like to be fed at the same time each day.

Do not overfeed your pet. You can prevent many health problems by keeping your dog lean. Provide a bowl filled with fresh, clean water. Offer healthy treats such as raw carrots or dog biscuits. Nylon bones can also help safely clean a dog's teeth.

THINGS THEY NEED

Springer spaniels welcome activity. These hunting dogs need room to roam. They cover ground rapidly in their search for game. **Bred** to retrieve from fields and streams, springer spaniels work in many settings.

Daily exercise is a must to keep your pet healthy and active. Springer spaniels enjoy competing in field trials. These trials test and score dogs on their ability to hunt, find, and retrieve game.

At home, this breed joins in on all outdoor activities. Spaniels especially love swimming! They enjoy long walks as well as playtime in a secure area. Keep your dog safe by attaching a collar tag

18

containing your address and phone number.

Indoors, springer spaniels will scope out their own special spot. A crate with a bed offers springers of any age the perfect place to snooze, travel, and keep toys. Puppies won't usually soil their dens, so crating also helps housebreak them.

If a springer spaniel is well trained, it will behave around people or other dogs.

PUPPIES

Springer spaniels are **bred** for the field, for shows, or just for people to adopt as pets. Mother dogs are **pregnant** for about 63 to 65 days. Medium-sized breeds give birth to an average of four to eight puppies in each **litter**.

Puppies are born blind and deaf. They spend most of their time sleeping, nursing, and growing. The puppies open their eyes and ears around two weeks of age. They can walk at three weeks. And, they are usually **weaned** by eight weeks of age.

Puppies are ready for adoption when they are between eight and ten weeks old. You can purchase a **purebred** springer spaniel from a qualified breeder. Or, visit a breed rescue or **Humane Society** to adopt springer spaniel puppies and older dogs.

Take your new springer spaniel to a veterinarian. Puppies will have had their first shots during their stay at the **breeder**'s. The veterinarian will continue these **vaccines** and check for worms. A healthy springer spaniel will live about 12 to 14 years.

Springer spaniels may guard their families well.
And, they are usually good with children.

GLOSSARY

American Kennel Club (AKC) - an organization that studies and promotes interest in purebred dogs.

breed - a group of animals sharing the same appearance and characteristics. A breeder is a person who raises animals. Raising animals is often called breeding them.

domestic - animals that are tame.

family - a group that scientists use to classify similar plants or animals. It ranks above a genus and below an order.

Humane Society - an organization that protects and cares for animals.

litter - all of the puppies born at one time to a mother dog.

muzzle - an animal's nose and jaws.

neuter (NOO-tuhr) - to remove a male animal's reproductive organs.

pregnant - having one or more babies growing within the body.

purebred - an animal whose parents are both from the same breed.

spay - to remove a female animal's reproductive organs.

vaccine (vak-SEEN) - a shot given to animals or humans to prevent them from getting an illness or disease.

wean - to accustom an animal to eat food other than its mother's milk.

WEB SITES

To learn more about springer spaniels, visit ABDO Publishing Company on the World Wide Web at **www.abdopub.com**. Web sites about springer spaniels are featured on our Book Links page. These links are routinely monitored and updated to provide the most current information available.

INDEX